THOUGHTS RUB IN

SOME IDEALISTIC THOUGHTS

MANIKANDAN CHANDRASEKARAN

Copyright © Manikandan Chandrasekaran
All Rights Reserved.

This book has been self-published with all reasonable efforts taken to make the material error-free by the author. No part of this book shall be used, reproduced in any manner whatsoever without written permission from the author, except in the case of brief quotations embodied in critical articles and reviews.

The Author of this book is solely responsible and liable for its content including but not limited to the views, representations, descriptions, statements, information, opinions and references ["Content"]. The Content of this book shall not constitute or be construed or deemed to reflect the opinion or expression of the Publisher or Editor. Neither the Publisher nor Editor endorse or approve the Content of this book or guarantee the reliability, accuracy or completeness of the Content published herein and do not make any representations or warranties of any kind, express or implied, including but not limited to the implied warranties of merchantability, fitness for a particular purpose. The Publisher and Editor shall not be liable whatsoever for any errors, omissions, whether such errors or omissions result from negligence, accident, or any other cause or claims for loss or damages of any kind, including without limitation, indirect or consequential loss or damage arising out of use, inability to use, or about the reliability, accuracy or sufficiency of the information contained in this book.

Made with ❤ on the Notion Press Platform
www.notionpress.com

This book I like to dedicate to my parents, friends, family, all inspirational people known and unknown.

Contents

Contents

Preface

This book contains some philosophical articles which I tried to write in my free time based on my readings. It is not intended to be a reference book or a complete guide to a way of life or my personal life. It is simply theoretical knowledge and some analytical discussion based on some interests. Thanks!

Acknowledgements

I like to thank my family members, my friends, people of my country and other inspirational people who have motivated me to try do something in life through learning or any other positive activity, while I had the motivation and aspiration but had less ideas This book might not be a big work on comparison with many other stalwart's writings. I have tried to base my writings on a positive or more neutral note on an analytical perspective.

Thought Experiments, Logic and Propositions

CHAPTER I

Trolley Problem- A thought experiment in philosophy

The Trolley Problem is a thought experiment where a user/an agent is in a decision-making scenario of either saving 'n' or saving 'n+m' (n, m>0) lives given a set of contrasting conditions in favor of the fewer number(n).

Scenario 1: Imagine there is a railway track that is bifurcated into 2, and the agent(you) is at a place where it is convenient to change the train track. One railway track has 5 children who are carelessly playing, and on the other track, there is one person walking towards his destination, knowing that there will be no train that will be crossing the track anytime soon. When the train comes, as a bystander, the agent doesn't have time to alert the 5 people, might/ might not know the intrinsic details, and has to take action based on instincts. What will be the course of action if he knows that in the course of saving 5 lives, he is going to kill an innocent person walking along the tracks, or if he doesn't take any action to change track, the 5 children will be killed? Saving 5 lives could be called 'utilitarianism'- the greater good for a greater number of people, whereas killing one person in the process could be called murder'- a categorical mistake, which might give a guilty conscience.

Scenario 2: Imagine the agent is standing on the railway platform, and 5 (new, naïve or expert) people are working on the tracks at some distance, and the agent is aware of it. A train is approaching, there is a fat man who is near the train on the platform, and there is no one else in the station, which means there is no one watching. If he is pushed directly by his hands, or there is some indirect switch mechanism, such as pushing the trolley on which he is resting, which will trigger the result of the fat man falling in front of the train that will make the train stop. Will the agent do the action, and which action will the agent prefer, or will the agent not prefer to take any action at all, resigning to fate (fatalism)?

The Trolley Problem is the scenario of taking the blue pill vs the red pill for protagonist Neo in *The Matrix*, where one pill is supposed to save his love interest and the other the people of the planet, to put it simply. There are plenty of such case scenarios in movies, perhaps in real life as well, and sometimes, they are played over and over again repeatedly, as the same set of events differently based on different sets of actions. In a way, the Trolley Problem could also be restated as being objective vs being subjective or, to put it in layman's terms, following the mind(reason) versus the heart (pride, emotion, intuition). The answers vary from person to person and need not be the same. It is to be noted that some problems do not require any necessary action simply because they are asked to choose. Inaction (not choosing) is also a choice, but nevertheless a difficult choice, for having to be the lone person in not joining a bandwagon.

Why not inaction? What if, in scenario 1, the train which is changed tracks collides with another train after some time or the track is not fully constructed, killing people in the train, saving 5 lives has cost many lives in the name of ignorance or the agent has the knowledge that if he performs that railway track changing action, he will be doing a penal offence and be punished severely, possibly hanged, leaving his family in a spot of financial bother. Will the agent still do the action and try to be humanitarian, which might go in his mind through bandwagon appeal (popularity) or respect for reason (rationality)? Over the course of time, he may well forget that incident and live happily if he hadn't rushed or acted hastily at that point in time.

A similar argument could be presented for scenario 2; the fat man can stand for the prejudice that the agent might have against certain kinds of people with certain features. Pushing the man directly with hands versus smartly pushing the trolley through legs or some other indirect trigger mechanism is going to have the same result, but if one life is to be sacrificed, the ultimate benefit of saving five lives will be taken as the end purpose, and the guilt conscience could be reduced by one action over another. Arguments could be presented in favour and against both actions, and henceforth, it is subjective, and no universal solution could be presented. The agent could feel morally right based on their beliefs; a trade-off has to be made. It is not possible to follow utilitarianism and avoid categorical mistakes in this problem. There have been various thought experiments both within philosophy and also in science, where, in order to explain concepts, certain abstractions were drawn out of the box. One such thought experiment is Schrödinger's cat, designed by Erwin Schrödinger in order to explain the quantum principle of how a live cat could behave in a quantum field. It is a hypothetical cat that is assumed to be both dead and alive at the same time, as it is unobserved within a black box when a quantum field is provided based on which its fate will be decided.

Further Readings:

1. Encyclopedias on the internet or internet search with terms 'Trolley Problem', 'Thought Experiment' and 'Schrödinger's cat' etc.

CHAPTER II

Paradoxes, Oxymorons and tongue twisters

"A good man cannot be altogether cheerful under old age and poverty combined, so on the other, no wealth can ever make a bad man at peace with himself." - Plato, The Republic.

A paradox might look like it is going to contradict itself, but actually it isn't. It is an oxymoron that cancels out itself. Let us see the definitions: According to the Oxford Learner's Dictionary, a paradox is a person, thing or situation that has 2 opposite features and, therefore, seems strange. An example cited there was, "He was a paradox—a loner who loved to chat to strangers." In philosophy, there are many paradoxes. There is the Catch-22 Paradox, Barber's Paradox, Raven's Paradox, Curry's Paradox, Liar's Paradox, Ship of Theseus Paradox and many more. The Catch-22 Paradox is, for example, when someone is in need of something, it can only be had by not having it. An example cited is that a soldier who wanted to be declared insane to avoid combat will be deemed not insane for that very rationalism he exhibits. This Catch-22 Paradox could also be extended to monks, who, in order to understand the world, have to renounce the very world that they live in. A Liar's Paradox is if a person says, "I am from a place where people always speak lies," or "This sentence is false," How are they to be trusted and proceed? Curry's Paradox is a claim that is asserted based on an arbitrary condition. For example, if India wins the cricket match against West Indies today, then China borders India. The antecedent (the first part before it) will have no relation to what follows if(consequent). Also, the consequent need not always be true; it could be a false statement as well. The Barber's Paradox is, "A male barber shaves all and only those men who do not shave themselves. Does he shave himself?" The Ship of Theseus Paradox is based on Greek history: "If all the parts of Theseus' famous ship are replaced one by one over a period of time, is it still the original famous ship?" It could be extended to a man and his belief system as well.

Having listed some paradoxes, oxymorons can be defined. An oxymoron is a figure of speech that has two contradictory words put together side by side but is meaningful. For example, a pretty ugly, wise fool, awfully good, cruel kindness, found missing, clearly misunderstood, definitely maybe, alone together are some oxymorons. Thus, it could be summarised as follows: all oxymorons are paradoxes, but not all paradoxes are oxymorons. There are tongue twisters, which are grammatically correct, difficult to spell continuously for more times without slipping, and are used in alliterations in speech therapy to improve pronunciation and fluency by repeating the same letter more times (alliterations).

Ex:

1. Peter Piper picked a peck of pickled peppers.
A peck of pickled peppers Peter Piper picked.
If Peter Piper picked a peck of pickled peppers,
Where's the peck of pickled peppers Peter Piper picked?

2. Betty Botter bought some butter
But she said the butter's bitter
If I put it in my batter, it will make my batter bitter
But a bit of better butter will make my batter better

References:

1. vocabulary.com
2. Oxford learner's dictionary
3. Wikipedia

CHAPTER III

Types of logical fallacies and can I live in a fallacy free world–a fantasy?

Fallacies are mistakes that happen when unsound reasoning or faulty reasoning occurs.

Straw Man Fallacy

This fallacy occurs when the opponent over-simplifies or misrepresents the argument presented by a person (thereby setting up a "straw man"). Instead of fully addressing the actual argument, speakers relying on this fallacy present a very similar — but ultimately unequal — version of the real stance, thereby defeating the argument.

Example 1:

Person 1: A person should vote in order to exercise his rights in a democracy.

Person 2: Whoever doesn't vote is acting against democracy and doing grave injustice to society.

Example 2:

Person 1: The movie has the same old formula

Person 2: You are saying it is a waste of time?

Bandwagon Fallacy

This fallacy occurs when a majority of the population agrees with an opinion, thereby making the minority of the population agree. Example: Popularity, media and opinion. While most expect to see bandwagon arguments in advertising (e.g. out of 10 people think X brand does the work best"). "He is the best person in the whole world. I have not seen any charismatic person/leader before in my life. See, everyone agrees. What is wrong with you?"

Post Hoc Ergo Propter Hoc: This is a conclusion that assumes that if 'A' occurred after 'B', then 'B' must have caused 'A.' Ex: Physicians and hospital attendants of the 19th century in a particular hospital at one point in time were superstitious about the death of children in a hospital. They had the impression that the deaths were caused by the visit of a few religious people, which could be called the Post hoc ergo propter hoc fallacy. However, one physician said that the lack of sterilisation of needles was the reason for the unfortunate incident and helped formalise the process.

Genetic Fallacy: Here, if a fallacy occurs due to the attribution of something to someone or some reason, that has happened in the past at some point in time, it is called 'Genetic fallacy'. Ex: I have erred; therefore, I will always err. The Nazis and the modern German cars have some mysterious connection.

Begging the Claim Fallacy: Here, rather than sound reasoning, what is to be proved will be presented as an argument. Thereby, people might agree. Ex: In comedy shows, a woman character might argue with her partner for fun, "You can obviously see I am right." even though she very well knows otherwise. On a serious note, a senator might argue for clean energy by presenting facts or through a begging the claim fallacious argument, by presenting, 'Polluting coal should be banned', or a person could claim himself to be a messenger and believe that truth because he likes to believe that truth, for which's disproval if people question the proof, he has to present proofs necessitated by the people.

Circular Argument: Here, two propositions are presented, one of which is presented as true because of the presence of another. Ex: Mineral water is healthy because it has minerals, and it is mineral-rich because it is healthy.

Either/Or Fallacy: Here, two choices are presented as the only options, where the author ignores a range of choices. **Ex:** Not owing a car and owning a car can be presented as the only options ignoring rental plans for a community.

Ad Hominem Fallacy: Here, the speaker attacks the character of the person rather than the argument of the person, undermining the argument. Ex: Senator 1: Clean energy is what is required for the state, country and the world. A law should be passed so that equality prevails. Senator 2: He is a corrupt and dishonest person. No words of him should be taken seriously.

There are many more fallacies, and if a question is asked, can I live in a fallacy-free world, where perfection is the epitome, it might be said as a dream cum true, which could again be a fallacy when compared with the first world, where it could be argued that happiness has prevailed through some order, whether through fallacies or some form of truth, than self-proclaimed truth, which everyone may not be able to achieve and may not be the correct version of how the world operates.

References: Internet various sources

CHAPTER IV

Propositions, Set Theory, Logic Gates, Genetic Algorithms and Categorization

Doubtless some philosophers have had all sorts of wisdom except common sense - Will Durant

In thePhilosophy of Logic, propositions are statements, some truths or negativity about truths, confirming the bias.

President Mr. Kennedy was assassinated. - Assertion/ Proposition-Truth. It could be stated as K, which means K is true.

A tilde or a hyphen in front of K makes it a negation statement, which means K is not true.

P1: All great philosophers think extremely well.
P2: Mr. Socrates is a great philosopher.
C: Therefore, Mr. Socrates thinks extremely well.

In the above example, all three statements are propositions. The first two propositions (P1 and P2) are known as premises, forming the argument and the last proposition is the conclusion. This method of arriving at a conclusion, using two or more propositions as argument is called, 'Syllogism'. P1 is a universal proposition and hence it is a major premise and P2 is a specific case and it is a minor premise.

The next step is the representation in mathematics through the Set theory. Symbols are indicated in brackets.

All($\forall$) great philosophers(X) are present such that all are(belongs to $\in$ good thinkers(T)) and Mr. Socrates(S) belongs($\in$) to the class of great philosophers(X) and therefore($\therefore$) he is a good thinker.

It could be represented as:
$\forall X/\ X{\in}T, S{\in}X, \therefore\ S{\in}T$

The same could be represented in terms of BASIC or any computer programming logic through if-else statements. In higher order, logic gates with AND combinations and further neural networks or genetic algorithms, based on training data provided and score matching, best fit, respectively. It could be simplified as the world works on the incremental logic system from a lower order to a higher order, and it has worked chronologically over the centuries. The same could be said of Aristotle's classification of first principles, ontology into categories and then the categories expanded to various branches of science- zoology, botany, physics, chemistry, and genetics, and has formed the basis of Database Management Systems (DBMS) as well. Last but not least, propositions come in everyday life, whether it could be part of the sentences uttered (speech), movie titles, song lyrics, etc, but one can't keep track of all the things that are said and done by him on a day to day basis. All one can do is keep track of life by avoiding problems/confusion and leading a healthy lifestyle or lifestyle of choice, which is very well known and could be called 'truism' or a 'cliché', whichever category the statement fits.

Fusional Writings

This section will cover some basic own writings of mine based on fusion of various concepts.

CHAPTER V

Infinite regress, past life regression and an infinite logic loop in mathematics– An analogy

Past life regression is a method in hypnosis to recover what practitioners believe are past lives or incarnations. [1] An infinite regress is a series of related elements with a first member but no last member, where each element leads to or generates the next in some sense. [2] It could simply be said that they are both related or similar. Hypnosis and the method through which one member leads to another is the thread in both these concepts, and the memories and members could be said to be flowers. So, in a way, it could be said that they both are related. What could the weaving of the members of the memories lead to? It could lead to a beautiful garland that the person may like or dislike. Past life regression might be a huge step which could lead to uncertainties in the present life if undertaken wrongly. There might be many beautiful memories or small moments that might have been cherished on a day-to-day basis, but only a few remain in the mind. If only one activity is undertaken steadfastly, only that activity remains in the mind. It could be any activity: cycling, thinking, studying, mixing one thing with another (confusion), etc. An example of a finite regress in a past life that could be stated is *The Butterfly Effect*, in which the protagonist fixes the problem that he faced as a child through a positive thought process or different approach over a period.

Virtue, the embodiment of elevated moral principles, stands in stark contrast to vice, defined by its wicked and immoral behavior. This dichotomy draws a parallel to the very essence of regress, which not only gives birth to a continuous journey but, paradoxically, also leads to potential contradiction. [2] In the case of infinite regress in general in philosophy, an example cited is Plato's Theory of Forms, where if two things are similar in nature, sharing certain similar features, then they may have more things in common, leading to infinite regress. [2] It is argued that this is a vice, a wicked or immoral thing, as infinite pondering/search is being conducted with no proper knowledge and sometimes the perception of the stability of an object, thing, life or mind, in general, is getting affected in the process. Anything could be similar to any other form of object in one aspect or another. The argument could be made simpler wherein a computer programming language is asked to do a task, such as print numbers in an infinite loop statement, and it never stops. It continues to print numbers, and only the user gets sick or tired of it, and he considers that as gibberish after its amusement period is over. An analogy that could be drawn is the computer with the user's mind, the sequence printed with the memories, which could be any type: incremental, decreasing, alternating, etc. Just as a skilled gardener tends to a garland's blooms, the mindful navigation of these interconnected concepts can lead to personal growth, while undue probing might result in disarray. This viewpoint underscores the importance of recognizing the limits of exploration and respecting the well-being of the one who explores along with the people around.

References:

1. Wikipedia
2. Stanford's Encyclopedia of Philosophy
3. Edited some portions with the help of https://chat.openai.com/

CHAPTER VI

Individualism vs Collectivism in a person's life

Definitions:

Individualism is a social theory favouring freedom of action for individuals over collective or state control.

Collectivism is the practice or principle of giving a group priority over each individual in it.

"Many hands make work light" is a proverb which stresses on collectivism. Individuals who work with others have each other as backup and try to reach their goals. It takes time, effort, and focus to do so. An aspiring writer, a painter, a musician or a craftsman, for that matter, will require their own space in order to mould their works. An individual might have benefitted from society, and it is stressed that it is his obligation to give something back to society; societies work based on trust, motivation and aspirations. An individual might have learnt something new from some sources, for example, public speaking, writing in English/Tamil or some sort of belief, but the source may not be the intended medium of education. So, by individualism, the individual's actions should be favoured, as it could be argued that he has found his path of light of living life happily and simply. It is to be noted that he lives with others, not alone. In big, reputed companies and Multi-National Companies (MNCs), teamwork is much appreciated, and appraisals are given by the team managers. Without teamwork, an individual cannot succeed in completing the project. Without anyone at the side of an individual, there comes a question of who will cry if the individual dies. An individual can try to accomplish many things and various activities in his lifetime, justifying in the name of utilitarianism, which is the ultimate good in the end, benefitting many people. There have been many successful people who would have succeeded in doing impossible tasks, but an unambitious, untrained, hard-working person with some desires/ideas may not be able to accomplish all the desires even if presented with the opportunities, as the desires could be called vague manifestations of the mind. Then, there is the concept of being objective rather than having subjective experiences. The balance of objectiveness and subjectiveness is important. Objective reality alone may not help a person succeed completely. Is there something wrong when a person is herded and taken care of with basic necessities by a caretaker who knows the affairs of the world?

If a person wishes to be herded and taken care of at one point but attributes his arrested development to the very same desire, rather than taking the blame, he forgets and puts the blame on the other side. So, he likes collectivism with fewer individual desires. He feels he has grown with big responsibilities and wants to put things in order, but he is unable to do so due to some factors. He is ambitious towards showing off his mettle and strengths and getting appreciated by the world, but the hard work and attention to detail that he has to present cannot be obtained from all the data that he absorbs in the world. He may feel he is neither obligated to anyone, nor is anyone obligated to him, but if a sense of duty is instilled, he might, as an individual, feel obligated to help the society or his family members who have helped him or shaped his career. To quote Dr. A. P. J. Abdul Kalam, "Where there is righteousness in the heart, there is harmony in the house; when there is harmony in the house, there is order in the nation; when there is order in the nation, there is peace in the world." It could be stated as an idealistic, over-ambitious statement, but it could also refer to some form of truism on how a person behaves and conducts his affairs will most likely make up his whole world. Harmony in a house and order in the nation may not be causally connected via arrow and head diagram, but through some chaos theory, such as the flip of a butterfly wing, things could be connected. So, even though an individual may not favour collectivism(or other forms such as communism or socialism, where a group is given priority in one form over the individual because of his lack of knowledge or other reasons) directly, he could try to get the favours, at least for his family members, a collectivistic approach, thereby preventing them from undergoing any peril.

CHAPTER VII

Eating pancakes and Lama-ism

Like in maths, x=y or 'peaches' as a code word for Manny in the Ice Age-3 movie or Dalai Lama's allusion to something to coffee, this essay will have 'eating pancakes' for some phenomena. It is to be remembered that I am not referring to anything in particular with absolute certainty. It could refer to any of the rules and regulations that exist in one country and not in another. Eating pancakes can even be described as something that could be based on appetite in one country but ritualistic in another. Therefore, it could be said to be part of a belief system in one place and a normal thing in another. It could also be said that things were different before and have progressed over the years.

Let's say Peter X is from one land/age. How his mind processes the data (in a computer matrix model), if it is not only pancakes but also plenty of other phenomena, differs is what the following content is about:

The mind gets confounded and confused about how to process the data initially, as there are two contrasting sets of data and relationships loaded.

If a computer program takes a certain time to multiply a 3X3 matrix, what can the mind do with, say, 100 or 1000 rows of data and relationships stored in an E-R schema in the mind database?

It could try to commit one set of action as per one schema and expect results of positive nature. If the results confer, mind exists in a defined schema, can be said to have kept things or affairs in order. But if it flaunts rules, it could get excited that life has opened some new possibilities. A new portal or schema could have been said to be launched.

It could possibly question why such a matrix model exists in land/age one and then rationalise that it is kept as part of different data definitions, which could be called culture sacred or order.

A new free will could get develop based on the definitions. How far that free will is agreeable or good nature or a saleable commodity in the world is a different question. What does multiplying A with A inverse do in a matrix, gives 1, an identity. A man could said to get his identity through this process.

CHAPTER VIII

Number systems – Ancient and Computer Age

Number systems have moved from the use of fingers and tally marks (ex: 1111 for 4, 11 for 2) to the use of sets of glyphs(specific shape or design) able to represent any conceivable number efficiently.[1] Octal systems involved the use of 8 as a base, hexadecimal the use of 16 as a base, ternary with 3 as a base, sexagenary the base 60, and so many more. This article is a quick summary of how addition and multiplication work for different number systems. Unary is a basic natural number with the base as 1, and it is different from other systems as it does not involve 0. Base or radix is defined as the number of unique digits in that system, including zero. Binary has 0 and 1 as the digits; ternary has 0, 1 and 2 as the digits; octal has 0-7, and decimal has 10 from 0-9. For a computer science graduate, how the system works and how the multiplication table works, the person might be familiar with the systems. For those people, this article is just a quick revision of some history, number equivalents, multiplication where these systems are used, and all others. It will be information worth reading.

If in decimal, 1+1 is 2, 1+3 is 4, since binary has 0,1 as the numbers, 1+1 is denoted by 10, which is the equivalent to 3 as 10 comes after the first two binary numbers 0 and 1. Other arithmetic operations work similarly, except the numbers corresponding change. For ternary, octal systems the operations work similarly, the symbols or notations differ.

So, where does each number system work? Following are with respect to ancient civilisations: Proto-cuneiform(Mesopotamia), Babylonian, and Sumerian numerals had 10(decimal) & 60(sexagenary) as a base, Egyptian, Indian, Greek, Hebrew and many other systems had 10(decimal) as the base, Mayan had 5 &20 as their decimal. Apart from the known number systems of octal, hexadecimal, and binary used in computing, there are systems like quadravigesimals with base 24(comprising numbers 0-9 and alphabets A), used in 24-hour timekeeping and also there are non-integer bases, negative bases and even complex bases.

For more information:
Please read any encyclopedia for number systems or relevant text material.

CHAPTER IX

Gestalt Psychology, Logo Design and Outliers

Gestalt is a German word meaning 'form' or 'configuration'. Gestalt psychologist's primary focus was perception, and they believed that organisms perceive perceptions as entire and not on individual parts. [1] They believed that perceptual experiences depend on the patterns formed by stimuli and on the experience of organisation. [2]

For example, in a figure, all there will be present are dotted lines, but the mind rushes to conclude that it is of some geometric figure. Below is an example: -------. Mind tends to conclude the figure as a straight line when in fact, it is a dotted line. The same could be said for a square or a circle, based on the experience of organising and classification.

Gestalt psychology was developed in response to school of structuralism in psychology. Structuralism analyzes basic thoughts and feelings, that combined to create complex phenomena in the mind. Logos of companies have also been designed based on Gestalt psychology. CNBC, hp computers, apple logos can be said to be inspired from Gestalt psychology.

In an investigation, with missing pieces of information, if one tends to go with the obvious suspect with the obvious motive, based on experience, then it could be stated that it is Gestalt psychology, though advanced computer training methods such as Artificial Neural Networks, Machine Learning Model could also be used, wherein the outliers tend to get omitted by the system.

References:

1. Wikipedia
2. Introduction to Psychology by Atkinson
3. https://userpeek.com/blog/what-are-gestalt-principles/
4. http://www.usertesting.com/resources/topics/gestalt-principles

CHAPTER X

What young India needs? Fictional, Incremental and Strategic

Dr APJ Abdul Kalam, in his book *India 2020* and Chetan Bhagat *What Young India Wants*, had two different visions about India. In Tamil cinema, there are lyricists like Vaali and Vairamuthu who have written dream songs with beautiful nature and language beyond imagination. For example, in the movie Amarkalam, the hero sings, "I wanted this, that for four minutes and finally laments nothing I got. Is life that painful for some? In *Thiruda Thiruda*, in a melodious song, the heroine and the hero together sing, "I want golden rain, cuckoo singing in Tamil..."

Dr. Amartya Sen argues in this book, *The Argumentative Indians*, about the historical incidents of how Indians have tried to debate various matters over the centuries through reason. So, can it be argued, Indians are fierce debaters and like to give counter arguments, in spite of having overwhelming evidence against them? So, Indians are rationalists. They go with reason. If evidence is presented to them, they try not to accept it initially but, later on, accept it. Does India need peace, justice, truth, and equality for all, or does it need personal simple life, pure in its own way, without any confusion/complications, a job, a simple materialistic lifestyle combined with a good, beautiful mind, some simple milestone achievements, some good people to interact with lifetime, even though in a way speaking it looks like a herd mentality(there is nothing wrong with it and it is, in fact, better than the fact of having been left alone)? What does young India want? A playful, enjoyable and memorable past and future? Some milestone achievements include getting into a respectable company, living with some family pride and dignity, showing bravery in times of need, and wisdom/

caution in other times. A healthy body, a healthy lifestyle/mind and a happy family? According to Chetan Bhagat, since the above are basic criteria, he goes on to cleaner airports, neat toilets and many more. A political party like the Aam Aadmi Party may have different aspirations from those of socialism. Dr APJ Abdul Kalam's book has the following chapters,

Can India Become a Developed Country?

What other countries Envision for Themselves

Evolution of Technology Vision 2020

Food, Agriculture and Processing

Materials and the Future

Chemicals Industries and Our Biological Wealth

Manufacturing for the Future

Services as People's Wealth

Strategic Industries

Health Care for All

The Enabling Infrastructure

Realizing the Vision

Response Towards India

It is a strategic book, and also there are planning committees and elected representatives, who care full time about the goals that are to be achieved. Separating fiction from facts, noise from signal, workable from unimplementable can the minds that are ignited help achieve worthy goals?

CHAPTER XI

Dionysian/ Apollonian – Life in Black and White?

In Greek mythology, Apollo and Dionysus are both sons of Zeus, just like King Dhritarashtra (son of Ambika) and King Pandu (son of Ambalika) are half sons of Vyasa Rishi. Zeus, Apollo, and Dionysus were all considered gods in Greek times. Apollo, son of Leto, is the god of the sun, art, music, poetry, plague and disease, rational thinking and order, appeals to logic, prudence and purity, and stands for reason. (Courtesy: Wikipedia) [The reason for NASA choosing Apollo as the name for the moon mission programme on its website is the image of "Apollo riding his chariot across the sun seemed appropriate to the grand scale of the proposed programme." and also might have something to do with the god himself, a rationally planned mission].

Dionysus, son of Semele, is the god of wine, dance and pleasure, of irrationality and chaos, representing passion, emotions and instincts. (Courtesy: Wikipedia). Whether they form part of the same entity or are different gods is a different matter of debate. In the current day scenario in 2023 AD, in Tamil Nadu and in India, there are different deities; gods are given the role of giving the blessings that the devotees ask for with pure intentions. Among the blessings, couples might ask for a child (fertility for the family tree to grow). If tantric practices are to be considered Dionysian, they are mostly separated from temple worship (except for some rare festivals like Ambubachi Mela/Ameti in goddess Kamakhya's temple in Assam- based on Wikipedia readings and understandings), and the Dionysian methods of madness in life mostly may not help meet the end goals of life. So they say, in life, everything needs to be balanced.

E: Is God eternal? (lasts forever) T: Is God temporal? (relating to worldly as opposed to spiritual) C: Is God conscious? (aware of and knows one's surroundings) K: Does God know the world? (as such, everything is happening everywhere) W: Does God include the world? (is the world part of God) (based on Stanford's Encyclopedia of Philosophy).

Apollonian and Dionysian are contrasting forces with one another, and if they are taken as some reference markers(dyes) in an Affymetrix microarray protein expression test chip, then they would glow brightly in their respective colours. Normal human life, which was mentioned as something that could be kept in balance, would be a combination of the two colours.

This theory of opposites can be extended to science and philosophy. In Chinese philosophy, yin-yang is described as an opposite, interconnected concept. In Chinese cosmology (a study dealing with the nature of the universe), the universe creates itself out of a primary chaos of material energy (a concept from the Greek philosopher Heraclitus), organised into the cycles of yin and yang and formed into objects and lives. Yin is the receptive and yang the active principle, seen in all forms of change and difference, such as the annual cycle (winter and summer), the landscape (north-facing shade and south-facing brightness), sexual coupling (female and male), the formation of both men and women as characters, and sociopolitical history (disorder and order). It could even be extended to the NDTV programme 'Left, Right and Centre', Hegel's 'Thesis, Antithesis and Synthesis', and the Dipole moment created within atoms in molecules due to differences in charges. How yin-yang differs from Samkhya's philosophy and much more will be discussed in some other articles.

CHAPTER XII

A brief introduction to abstract algebra and some analogies

This essay is about abstract algebra. What is abstract? The abstract exists in thought or as an idea but does not have a real existence. Algebra is a field where notations are used to represent quantities and do calculations. So, abstract algebra could be said to be a field where thoughts or ideas are tried to be expressed algebraically. So, when does a student start with abstract concepts in life? As early as a child, when new meanings are attached to life. These could be labelled psychological terms as interactionism of learning or others. As a student, he might have been introduced to abstract algebra when he passed 8th standard matriculation(Indian syllabus) or, in general, high school would have come across set theory. Sets are, in general, a group of elements and could be labelled A, B, C, etc. In a set introduction, A is usually said to be mapped with B, and the function that maps A to B may be called a one-to-one function. There are various types of mapping, such as to-one, onto, into, etc., and in other terms, they could be surjective (one-to-one and onto) or injective (one-to-one). In other words, if A interacts with B through a mechanism that could be expressed mathematically, then it could be called a composition of function. In real life, a forest officer or a bird watcher may know a species of bird through its sounds, or a person may know how his family members react to each situation. They could be called one-on-one mapping. In Bachelors mathematics, he might come across this as a separate subject. There, he will come across concepts such as groups, fields, rings, homomorphism, isomorphism, theorems, etc. Groups, fields and rings could be called algebraic structures. Groups could be said to be sets which have a single binary operation defined upon two sets, and the mapping could be anything like one-to-one, onto, into, etc., along with closure, an identity element and a corresponding inverse element. In real life, a person might have an identity(an ego) based on beliefs, and it does not have a concrete existence. There are various forms of groups, such as semigroups and quasi-groups, where one or more of the three properties mentioned (closure, identity, inverse) might not be there. Rings and fields are higher-order forms where two binary operations are defined(addition and multiplication). If a multiplicative inverse is not present and it need not be commutative, it is a ring, and if it is present, it is a field (except for zero multiplicative inverse). A homomorphism is a structure-preserving map(a function that could be expressed mathematically) between two algebraic structures(groups, fields, rings, etc.) of the same type (group 1 to group 2 and field 1 to field 2, etc.) Isomorphism is an algebraic structure-preserving concept which can be reversed by inverse mapping. It is also between two algebraic structures of the same type. It has a one-one correspondence between elements of the sets that preserves binary relations between elements of the sets. In real life, if a community, a society, or a family lives in unity, they could be analogous to algebraic structures. And each religion could also be taken to be some sort of algebraic structure. If it is taken as in a person's life, emotions and reactions such as fear, desire, and wishes could be called functions that might preserve his life or ego intact or might even destroy it by mapping to something negative or undesirable in life.

CHAPTER XIII

An analogy between music, painting and some concepts in math – Gödel, Escher and Bach by Douglas Hofstadter

Music has its own compositions, and they start with notes. Painting has its own compositions, starting with strokes. Maths, too, has its basics and compositions. In music, a fugue is a compositional technique that involves the systematic imitation of a main theme or subject in simultaneously sounding melodic lines. The term fugue can also refer to a work or part of a work that uses counterpoint between voices. In paintings, compositional types are called art movements. The type of paintings that involve symmetry and reflection, similar to maths, fall under that art movement. Systematic imitation of a main theme in music could be viewed in terms of symmetry in painting. Maths could be viewed in terms of symmetrical objects/shapes. In simplicity, even numbers can be viewed in terms of patterns when they come as sequences. Known sequences are incremental sequences that increment by a number, such as normal and natural numbers, Fibonacci sequences, and Lucas sequences. Sequences also occur when there is a recurrence in relation, and a function can define them. For example, if 1, 1, 2, 3, 5, 8, 13 are Fibonacci sequences, defined by $x(n) = x(n-1)+x(n-2)$, where 0+1=1, 1+1=2, 2+1=3, etc. and Lucas sequences are defined similar to Fibonacci sequence, except for different starting values. 2,1,3,4,7,11 etc. More complex types of sequences are also present. If musician Bach had composed some excellent fugues, Escher could have used recursion to create some recursive figures, which are a part of the conceptual art movement. Below is a work called *Tesselations* by Maurits Cornelis Escher (MC Escher), where recursiveness is outlined in black and white colours. He also paints an infinity staircase. Many artists have recently popularised conceptual art based on recursive relationships. Even Gestalt psychology, which was one of the chapters in this book (chapter 33), could be said to have a recursive relation, similar to Escher's paintings. The book *Gödel, Escher and Bach's An Eternal Golden Braid* covers these concepts. Gödel doesn't have any sequence in his name, except he proved the concept that not all mathematical concepts are provable in a well-defined mathematical system by using a recursive relationship in a maxim(a derived mathematical statement) defined from axiom(definitions), which could speak of itself(self-referencing) as false. In modern terms, a computer can be asked to print a statement, "I am a stupid machine," through a programming language, and it will do so. So, not everything is complete, be it in mathematics (Gödel's incompleteness theorems) or computers.

CHAPTER XIV

How to remember certain constants such as Euler's number(e) and pi?

There are universal constants, such as pi (π) and Euler's number (e), which have values with more digits after the decimal place. e=2.718281828459045...and π=3.14159265359. In order to remember the first few digits of such constants, various mnemonic techniques are used. For example, in order to remember Euler's constant(e), Jackson was an American president. He (2) was the seventh (7) president of America, and he was elected in 1828 (twice).The 20 USD bill in which his image was printed can be folded at an angle of 45-90-45 to form a boat. e=2.718281828459045 can be used to remember the constant value. π value is huge, and there are various world and Limca book holders who have successfully remembered using mnemonics the value post decimal and entered the records. Here, a simple mnemonic is shared, wherein, "Can I have a large container of coffee right now?" (3.141592653- Each word's letter count). Mnemonics can also be used to remember discrete random objects. For example, if a broomstick, table, cycle, bike, gold, tube light, or pen are given. A story or a sentence can be woven around those objects. While the servant was using a broomstick to clean the table, Ram used his cycle, as his bike didn't work well to get gold; with the tube light's lighting, he was able to write with the pen to present it as a gift to the servant. The significance of Pi and Euler's number can be searched on the web and in books. It is said that the Guinness record holder for remembering the most digits in pi has used some simple syllables such as ru, ra, and ri for each digit, which has some meanings in the language.

CHAPTER XV

Citizen Journalism, Online Petitions and Letters to the Editor

Citizen Journalism(CJ) works based on the concept of reporting by citizens on some particular topics of interest; it may be a eulogy(praising someone highly) or complaints/problems/issues in a locality, or it could be some personal experience supposed to be shared with a group of people, motivating others or the authority to take some sort of action on that particular issue. Private citizens, too, sometimes get together to solve that issue. Responsible, respected social welfare club meetings, local events, classifieds, and meetups could come up in CJ.

Online petitions (ex:change.org) are petitions asking for some change or reform. People start petitions for different reasons and on various matters. If enough people sign a petition, then the petition is handed over to an authority, mentioning the number of signatures and a need for action. An online petition is internet activism, whereas CJ is both internet and local activism in a way supporting decentralisation of power, highlighting the failures of power when it is vested with authority. There are other online activism groups, such as consumer complaint forums, and some companies voluntarily provide decent customer support, perhaps as long as this kind of effort is taken.

How about articles in the newspaper and letters to the editor? Only leading newspapers have some standard of journalism and some standard of ethics, and their voices are meaningful. Those newspapers have the option of asking their readers to write letters to them, perhaps on editorial articles or issues that concern them. Not all letters to the editor are published, and when the standards of publishing go below expectations, perhaps due to the arms strangling by the authorities or other reasons, can writing letters to the editor help, or will they get published? Similarly, when the internet is being manipulated, can the CJ work? Where will life move? To whom should one complain on both occasions? Only depend on centralised power? Which could be hell, as shown in movies, if there is corruption. One who doesn't know how to fight, against whom the fight should be, then simply has to be content with living life like a nomad, spiritual, grace of others, Slavic mindset or, to put it simply, a depressing scenario.

CHAPTER XVI

Ideas enter the mind and they click!

Definitions:

Truism – a statement that is obviously true and says nothing new or interesting

Epiphenomenalism is the view that mental events are caused by physical events in the brain but have no effects on any physical events. (Courtesy: Stanford's Plato)

Idealism in modern philosophy is something mental (the mind, spirit, reason, will) is the ultimate foundation of all reality, or even exhaustive of reality, and although the existence of something independent of the mind is conceded, everything that we can know about this mind-independent "reality" is held to be so permeated by the creative, formative, or constructive activities of the mind (Courtesy: Stanford Encyclopedia)

Aphrodite – Greek goddess of sexual love and beauty.

Viscosity is the resistance of a fluid (liquid or gas) to a change in shape or movement of neighbouring portions relative to one another. Viscosity denotes opposition to flow. (Courtesy: Britannica Encyclopedia).

The density of a liquid is a measure of how heavy it is for the amount measured.

Pragmatist- a person who is guided more by practical considerations than by ideals/ (in philosophy) an advocate of the approach that evaluates theories or beliefs in terms of the success of their practical application.

Epicureanism is a system of philosophy founded around 307 BC based upon the teachings of the ancient Greek philosopher Epicurus. Epicurus was an atomic materialist who followed the steps of Democritus. (Courtesy: Wikipedia)

Eccentricity – Unconventionality(slight deviation from convention), strangeness

Culture medium – solid, liquid, or semi-solid designed to support the growth of a population of microorganisms or cells via the process of cell proliferation

Microbial strain – A particular variety of a microbe
Phases of the bacterial growth curve – Lag phase, Exponential/ Growth phase, Stationary phase and Death phase(For more info, can refer to Wikipedia or any Microbiology book)

Eudaimonia – in Aristotelian ethics, the condition of human flourishing or of living well

Stoic – a student of ancient Greek philosophical school which practised 'virtue is sufficient for happiness' or 'virtue is the only good.'

A Virtue (Latin: virtus) is a trait of excellence that may be moral or intellectual. The cultivation and refinement of virtue is held to be the "good of humanity" and thus is valued as an end purpose of life or foundational principle of being. (Courtesy: Wikipedia)

Virtue ethics is currently one of three major approaches in normative ethics. It may, initially, be identified as the one that emphasises the virtues or moral character, in contrast to the approach that emphasises duties or rules (deontology) or that emphasises the consequences of actions (consequentialism) (Courtesy: Stanford Encyclopedia)

Overzealous and Passionate- Overzealous is showing too much energy or enthusiasm in pursuit of a cause or objective, and passion is having, showing, or being caused by strong feelings or beliefs.

Zenith – the time at which something is most powerful or successful.

THE ESSAY:

The title phrase was almost borrowed from the book *Allusions and Reflections* by Elisabeth Wåghäll Nivre. It is from the chapter titled 'Double Aphrodite and Her Reflections in Renaissance Philosophy.'

Idea as an external thought or suggestion:

Assuming ideas to be like the laminar (smooth or regular) flow(rather than turbulent flow) of a fluid in a pipe, they help a man to proceed with his actions, or even if a man does actions involuntarily/regularly, there must be some ideas that must come as input through auditory, visual, touch, taste and smell (five senses). In chemical engineering, the laminar flow rate in a pipe can be determined by calculating the flow at a small point or area and then integrating it for the full area of the pipe. Similarly, taking a single idea, I will try to proceed. How can it enter from an external source? It can come through an external medium (TV, radio, internet) or a social contact/circle (trusted and unknown). When the medium or the contact is trusted, ideas get reiterated (integrated form), or only desirable ideas get reiterated, and they quickly convert to actions. If there are different sets of ideas, it is like having different types of fluids flow in a pipe, and there will be viscosity (resistance) to the flow. Also, equally, how well each idea is flowing (the density) is to be considered. The analogy between the flow of a fluid and ideas ends here. Now, returning to the title, the title could be called a truism, at least with regard to my personal experience. It need not be detonated using the power of the individual; if the individual is able and well, the idea can click at any time. The scenario of an individual consciously trying to avoid that suggestion or idea is not workable. The maximum that the individual can do is try to avoid that idea by being strong and busy enough with another set of actions and ideas. As a result, over time, the individual will distance himself from its impact and forget about it.

What can an idea do to a person?

A person might remember or might have forgot that he had a suggestion from a source and carried out some actions and thereby becoming a habit.

2. By repeated reminders or eccentricity, he could constantly be thinking/wondering about that idea. The idea could be clogging the mind like a blood clot, and the source or similar, which had been the perpetrator, would term it as pathological nature of the psyche or some other medical term. For example, in negative case scenarios, a person might attribute the country's policies or failure of a relationship or might attribute the strictness or inefficacy of the educational institution for getting his life's energy sucked or having gotten below par education. If he is a pragmatist cum optimist (a kind of Epicureanism or eudaimonia), he proceeds on with life as if he still remains thinking of the past, it can have simply had moments of unhappiness, and he will like to have/enjoy at least other perks in life.

Assuming the mind to be like a culture medium(broth) in a bioreactor, containing ideas (microbial cells) under perfect conditions (willing recipient and right source for the idea), the ideas grow(proliferate), and then when the nutrients lacking or waste products accumulate (side effects), the ideas (like cells), just like microbes, ideas will stop growth and die. If it is something like a bioreactor, that is, someone taking care of the necessities and troubles of the mind, everything goes planned, i.e. there is no free will. The mind could be called an 'idea reactor'. The analogy for the mind may not be as perfect as a set of computer memories connected via a network, as shown in some movies like 'The Matrix' and also it is to be noted that each microbial cell has plenty of processes going on and getting a microbial strain is a painstaking process in itself. The final point that can be noted is that, like every kind of microbe (idea), every idea just will have a death phase. There is no talk/analogy of viruses that don't have a life outside but consume life when within.

Ideas that come from within:

Microbes can be found in different environmental conditions, and they are found in human digestive tracts. Some help in digestion, like probiotics. Similarly, ideas can occur under different environmental conditions, and they need not be only input signals; they can be inferences (outputs) as well. And when they are sent in again to the system (mind), it forms a kind of signal device. If the signals get amplified, the mind behaves in a way like an amplifier and reacts in a way it might not intend. There is repentance/ apology, a distraction, or a longing for knowledge/improvement. While I write this, I would like to mention Shiv Khera's words in *You Can Win!*: "The tragedy is that there are many walking encyclopedias who are living failures." So, even though a signal failure doesn't mean life (mind) in itself is a failure or any writer for this matter is a success, it is often times getting projected onto the mind through sources unconsciously.

If having a counselling session with a psychiatrist is projected as desirable and knowing different disease names is sometimes projected as desirable for proper diagnosis and prognosis (ideas), based on my understanding from watching movies/internet (source), then If I reiterate those ideas or trust the source completely, I will believe in it, even though it need not be always the case scenario. Self-help in the first case and if fear of a disease prevails, prevention of certain events like eating and drinking habits and avoiding obsession with certain things (being overzealous) can also help, rather than expecting miraculous and chance outcomes. So, the idea is invalidated. Can this wisdom be obtained by thinking through pure speculation and more consultation? Difficult, and it can only be obtained through practical experience.

Life need not be perfect and meaningful; this has been the message when I had many questions in college or in IT company; You need not be a student Vivekananda, looking in for Guru Ramakrishna nor become a fake saint either, in the process. It is to be noted that Vivekananda was a mendicant monk who became inspired and a guru. Not everyone can be enlightened (inspired or know some truth) and needs to be enlightened, but there is sometimes a thirst (trishna as in Buddhism) kindled somewhere mostly by the spirit (i.e. out of nowhere through curiosity) but could be blamed on a source, nevertheless (like reading a text, watching the news). But some enlightened are marketed as gurus/saints. These are some of the categories of saints/gurus: mendicant monks with materialistic lifestyles who believe in gurus or fake saints in India. Whether everyone is enlightened or correct is a question apart. So, something like the search for truth or some force like belief or idealism (perfection) drives everyone, and they settle finally in something called 'peace', 'mental calmness', 'ashram' or as a 'wrong advertisement for a guru'. Can being materialistic, altruistic (helping others), stoic (preaching virtue), disciplined, knowledgeable, and in the right mix succeed in the long run, or is a singular thing at its zenith desired? It's a question that I saw bewildering some people I know who discuss vigorously whenever some relevant news flashes. There is no doubt that an idea (belief or disbelief) has been self-detonated successfully!

CHAPTER XVII

Holism and Reductionism- Physiology and Molecular Biology

Systems biology is an approach in biomedical research to understanding the larger picture—be it at the level of the organism, tissue, or cell—by putting its pieces together. [1] Synthetic biology is a field of science that involves redesigning organisms for useful purposes by engineering them to have new abilities. [2] Proponents of systems and synthetic biology often stress the necessity of a perspective that goes beyond the scope of molecular biology (study of biology at a molecular level) and genetic engineering (modifying genes in an organism for a particular cause through various technologies), respectively. With an emphasis on systems and interaction networks, the approaches explicitly engage in one of the oldest philosophical discussions on reductionism vs. holism. [3] Reductionism in biology is a method of breaking down biological systems into their constituent parts to explain the chemical basis of living processes. It's a way of explaining things by breaking them down into smaller components. For example, biologists may study metabolism by looking at the structure of a cell. [4] Holism is the interdisciplinary idea that systems possess properties as wholes apart from the properties of their component parts. The aphorism "The whole is greater than the sum of its parts," typically attributed to Aristotle, is often given as a glib summary of this proposal. [5] Even in some calligraphic(handwriting techniques) arts, small words could be embedded to form larger words. This can be seen in the book, *Gödel, Escher and Bach* by Douglas Hofstadter or when one browses the internet with a tag cloud of words. Words could be formed by tagging a small number of words. If it is asked, without the smaller fonts, couldn't the bigger font be made? Yes, of course, it could be done with a few strokes. So, does physiology work better than molecular biology? Yes, but in a finer way, molecular biology works to give meaning to physiology. If the word 'life' (6) is searched on the internet, it could simply be made to look at many components like love, friendship, family, etc. These words could be beautifully embedded within the bigger word 'life'. Life is a holistic perspective, and all the smaller atomic words are reductionistic perspectives. So, in physiology and molecular biology (along with systems biology, synthetic biology and others), a similar argument could be presented. Medicines have been discovered from traditional sources, and medicines have also been discovered at the molecular level. A drug is called a blockbuster drug, as it takes around 10-15 years to bring the drug to the market. The reductionistic view helps in understanding complex phenomena at an intricate level that is unimaginable, with a level of detail like nanosciences. There are various organisms and living beings in the Tree of Life. As the complexity of life increases, interaction models vary, and a holistic approach from a reductionistic ground level in a deterministic manner is difficult. Reason and pain are simply parts of human life; how emotions interact and what results are produced vary from human being to human being and may not be present in other species and need not be understood for a normal being to live their life is the best analogy. This could be said of the existence of God or a noumenon (something abstract) and the various ways in which the abstract is said to be based.

References:

1. http://irp.nih.gov/
2. https://www.genome.gov/
3. https://plato.stanford.edu/entries/systems-synthetic-biology/
4. google.com (experimental AI view)
5. en.wikipedia.org
6. pinterest.com

CHAPTER XVIII

Justified True Belief(JTB), D-theory and Advaita

In philosophy, philosophers have often debated between knowledge and certainty. [1] A belief is said to be justified if people have enough reasons to believe in it. In the field of epistemology(the theory of knowledge), what constitutes a JTB has been a subject of debate. A popular example that is used for illustration is the cow in the field example, where a person mistakes a white cloth over an object in the field for his cow from a far away distance. These sorts of problems where a mistaken belief is truly believed are known as Gettier problems, as it was introduced by Edmund Gettier to show the fallibility of knowledge based on truth and belief as conditions. Various other conditions were introduced, and models developed to resolve this problem, such as no false belief condition (a belief cannot be based on a false belief, such as a watch that has stopped functioning but shows the correct time twice a day), causal connection condition (between knowledge and belief, there has to be a causal condition. If I believe in a medium/family/God has produced miracles or has protected/helped, and my life has changed, my belief will stay grounded on that part), conclusive reasons condition (as long as conclusive evidence points to certain facts, the person has to believe in those facts. There is a table in front of me, and it has been removed, as I can clearly see. I need not worry about it from the fourth dimension or any other scientific perspective, as it may not be known to me) and defeasibility condition(as long as the evidence is not pointing to the contrary, a belief is known. I believe in a god, and then because someone says there is no god, I cannot change my stance. It could be an accepted source of knowledge as per my belief system, a verbal testimony (a sabda), but still, it could also be by someone who knows me well and plays a small trick to test me, on an optimistic note). D-theory refers to defeasibility theory. If a person says a series of propositions loudly within himself with the belief that his thoughts are unreadable and, at one point in time, in an act of desperation, presents a defeasibility theory for uplifting his life or mode of thinking or testing or any other good/bad reason, then an augmented reality could be presented for that purpose. But will the person be steadfast in his approach, and will he be able to wither the storms that he has presented or artificially created, and how long can he survive in such hard/strenuous conditions, in spite of the best intentions of the entity on the other side? Will sanity prevail? This is often cited as one of the problems, say in some (for ex, cult, religion) groups, where a JTB is brought on a person, and that person tries to impart a JTB on another person through the methods he has learnt. The JTB may work but may not last or exist for a long time upon questioning and reasoning. The clarity, calmness, and thought process may be refined. Thus, in some cases, people may find it difficult to accept new members who are difficult to manage as their disciples because after reaping the benefits of having witnessed some miracles, they might spread misinformation or the negatives that were present in the group. The person may feel he succeeded, feel his problems are solved, and may present to lead a happy life on an outer scale, but there might be something pricking or missing in him that will be hard for him to replace, which might be an underlying reality. This could happen even if the person gets whatever world he desires. He could perceive one reality encoded on top of another. Advaita refers to perceiving one reality when that reality is superimposed on another underlying reality. Living with one reality is the way of life, as all underlying realities cannot be known immediately to senses, and this is the dictum that most people might follow. "Faith can move mountains" is a famous Biblical verse. If a question of "how much faith?" is asked, it could be said to depend on how big the mountains are and on what for and on what/whom I have placed the faith.

CHAPTER XIX

An Essay on Crime and Punishment

In school education, there are tales from Jataka and other fables where the moral of the story is asked to be inferred. Whoever has wicked plans, thoughts or actions loses, and the victor happens to be smart, calm, respected and the victorious. It could be a turtle, Chota Bheem, Jerry the mouse, Home Alone protagonist, Kung-fu Panda etc.

The next phase in life is in movie watching, where a bit of drama unfolds. The villain exists; he is bad, he does bad things, and he gets punished very badly in the end by the hero. Most popular movies have this theme. As long as it is a one-way communication and a belief formation, there are no issues. What if life presents with more villains through various mediums of communication, and the grown-up adult wonders, are there enough prison cells and why do so many come up in the first place? It is a pondering thought. Is there anything wrong with the thought? No, but sometimes all the villains could simply be imaginations. Say this character trait is not desired for this person; it is a villain.

In Plato's *The Republic*, a conversation is conducted on this topic. The question of whether laws are framed only with the interest of those in power; with the argument that an autocrat frames despotic laws, a democrat frames democratic laws and so on. So, by this it could be inferred that crimes and punishment do not have a complete correlation with one another. A guilty may not be punished at all. Does a guilty person need to be punished, and who is guilty? These sorts of questions come up. A person fighting an internal dilemma has thought crimes to his credit or men's rea, where the mental state of the defendant who has committed a crime is to be considered. The definition of guilt itself is inaccessible to the common man. What might have invoked capital punishment at one point in time might have had various revisions over the centuries, and a new imprisonment term might be in place in the current century.

Question: If a crime is not committed simply because of a fear of punishment, is the person guilty if a question is asked?
Answer: It is not a crime of serious nature.

Question 2: If a person keeps on thinking about some crime but does not commit a crime, which evokes bizzare responses from people around, based on his facial expressions, is a person guilty?
Answer: Whether guilty or not, the person might need psychiatric help, a consultation, or a new belief that works to boost confidence.

In current day democracy, vox populi (the voice of the majority) and courts, legal systems finds a way and the guilty are punished, even if the person is a ruling member, if data from news media are to be believed. In a dictatorship, aristocracy (ruled by king), autocrat (ruled by a strict ruler), oligarchy (ruled by a few people) however it might not be the case unfortunately.

Quotes, Anecdotes and a Poetic

This section contains quotes and anecdotes from some personalities in philosophy

CHAPTER XX

Quotes by John Stuart Mill(1806-1873)

It is indisputable that the being whose capacities of enjoyment are low has the greatest chance of having them fully satisfied, and a highly endowed being will always feel that any happiness which he can look for, as the world is constituted, is imperfect. But he can learn to bear its imperfections if they are at all bearable, and they will not make him envy the being who is indeed unconscious of the imperfections, but only because he feels not at all the good which those imperfections qualify.

It is better to be a human being dissatisfied than a pig satisfied; better to be Socrates dissatisfied than afool satisfied. And if the fool or the pig has a different opinion, it is only because they know their own side of the question.

From Utilitarianism

War is an ugly thing, but not the ugliest of things: the decayed and degraded state of moral and patriotic feeling, which thinks that nothing is worth a war, is much worse. When people are used as mere human instruments for firing cannons or thrusting bayonets in the service and for the selfish purposes of a master, such war degrades them. A war to protect other human beings against tyrannical injustice; a war to give victory to their own ideas of right and good, and which is their own war, carried on for an honest purpose by their free choice — is often the means of their regeneration. A man who has nothing which he is willing to fight for, nothing which he cares more about than he does about his personal safety, is a miserable creature who has no chance of being free unless made and kept so by the exertions of better men than himself. As long as justice and injustice have not terminated their ever-renewing fight for ascendancy in the affairs of mankind, human beings must be willing, when need is, to do battle for the one against the other.

From Principles of Political Economy

A person may cause evil to others not only by his actions but by his inaction, and in either case he is justly accountable to them for the injury.

On Liberty

He who knows only his own side of the case knows little of that. His reasons may be good, and no one may have been able to refute them. But if he is equally unable to refute the reasons on the opposite side, if he does not so much as know what they are, he has no ground for preferring either opinion... Nor is it enough that he should hear the opinions of adversaries from his own teachers, presented as they state them and accompanied by what they offer as refutations. He must be able to hear them from persons who actually believe them...he must know them in their most plausible and persuasive form.

Since every country stands in numerous and various relations with the other countries of the world, and many, our own among the number, exercise actual authority over some of these, a knowledge of the established rules of international morality is essential to the duty of every nation, and therefore of every person in it who helps to make up the nation, and whose voice and feeling form a part of what is called public opinion. Let not anyone pacify his conscience by the delusion that he can do no harm if he takes no part and forms no opinion. Bad men need nothing more to compass their ends than that good men should look on and do nothing. He is not a good man who, without a protest, allows wrong to be committed in his name and with the means which he helps to supply because he will not trouble himself to use his mind on the subject. It depends on the habit of attending to and looking into public transactions and on the degree of information and solid judgement respecting them that exists in the community, whether the conduct of the nation as a nation, both within itself and towards others, shall be selfish, corrupt, and tyrannical, or rational and enlightened, just and noble.

Inaugural address at the University of St. Andrews
Definition: tyrannical (exercising power in a cruel and arbitrary way)

In this age, the mere example of non-conformity, the mere refusal to bend the knee to custom, is itself a service. Precisely because the tyranny of opinion is such as making eccentricity a reproach, it is desirable that, in order to break through that tyranny, people should be eccentric. Eccentricity has always abounded when and where the strength of character has abounded, and the amount of eccentricity in a society has generally been proportional to the amount of genius, mental vigour, and moral courage that it contained. That so few now dare to be eccentric marks the chief danger of the time.

CHAPTER XXI

Story of a story - A poem

I didn't like stories,

Then I liked stories;

Then, always one plus one equals two stories

Then, suddenly, why not complex stories?

Entered fractals,

Then other territories,

Stories conveyed the same

In different dimensions and

Different geometries;

Perhaps happiness,

Perhaps motivation,

Perhaps life or whatever it is,

I might have been part of some story

Unknown to me.

I question an art or an artist

or say want to be part of something with half known details

How can a thing which could also represent a part of me in different dimensions or

Represent life in entirety in different proportions answer me or incorporate me as an entity that could help others,

Stories help

A child's imagination;

Give courage to speak in a world unknown

Give words

Give smartness

Give confidence

Give complex neural developments

Thought processes

And life develops well.

If life goes to complications when the child wants to play or take part in it via some live show and becomes a failure,

Stories could become one of the targets/ghosts;

It could be called an Imitation Game,

Merely a toy or a machine,

A reason for failure,

Merely some propaganda device.

When the question of why I like fractals rather than one plus one
equals two comes or

Why did my desire rather than ambition go one step higher comes
or even further,

Why did I like one plus one equals two in first place comes, I have
no answers.

If I can't remember all the stories, there could be nothing wrong,

If I can't tell a good story, there could be nothing wrong,

If I can't recollect some good stories, there could be nothing wrong;

But what could be wrong is,

when I blame a story or want a new story for my failed life which
could be

Due to some personal problems, misconceptions and failures of
mine,

Without knowing the full details,

A person who tells stories might know what life needs,

Stories help a bird's flight

As well it could help a caged bird at least remain happy

Alas it could even be a reason for it being caged!

- Authored by me, inspired by many

CHAPTER XXII

Nail in the fence – A short story

In a distant village, lived a young boy who had the problem of a fierce temper. Once, he happened to show his temper to his family while they were having dinner. The boy thought it was the best way of asserting himself in the world, and he saw nothing wrong by showing temper. A person should, after all, express his emotions and not confine things within himself. However, the father saw a problem with his attitude, as he thought that it was impossible to survive in the world by showing temperament. So, he devised an insightful lesson. Handing the boy a sack of nails, he instructed that every time anger overcame him, he was to drive a nail into the old wooden fence at the back of their yard.

The initial day saw the boy face various issues. He was unhappy with how things went. He didn't like the programme that ran on television, the news that he saw in the newspaper, the way his friends spoke regarding certain matters, the food that was prepared, the way he was treated by his sister and many others. He hit 40 nails into the fence out of frustration over a period of time. As weeks flowed by, a transformation unfurled. He asked his father if this was all necessary. What purpose does controlling one's temper do, as he could be treated like a waste by the world and he could do nothing about it? The father advised that it is the attitude or the way in which he expresses his opinion that matters. It will resolve the matters more quickly than prolonging a matter or bringing in a fight, which is hard to resolve. The boy's ability to rein in his temper grew, and the daily toll of nails that he hammered reduced gradually. The lesson was clear: managing his temper was simpler than driving those nails. But, there was still a question, an argument that was running that sprouted then and there: will he be able to succeed in life with the newfound attitude and how to express his opinions in times of desperation, if at all they come? Can he preach this wisdom or live with this among his friends?

Eventually, it could be said that a day arrived when the boy triumphed over his temper entirely, as he didn't drive any nails. It could be argued that he was tired of driving or bored of driving the nails if scepticism is allowed to reign. However, as per the story, he succeeded, and he shared his achievements with his father. In response, the father proposed that for each day the boy had controlled his anger, he should extract one nail from the fence. Time passed, and eventually, the boy stood before his father, proclaiming the fence nail-free.

Walking to the fence together, the father smiled gently at his son. "You've shown remarkable progress, my child. However, take a look at all the holes that have been left behind in the fence. Those marks, like wounds from spoken anger, linger on. A person, whether a fool or a genius, will remember things and even might act against you. You can't protect yourself from the world, no matter how hard you try! This is a simple fact. If you speak against a religion, you hurt the people who have faith in that religion. If you speak against a country, you hurt the people who live in that country. As a family member, I can forgive and might not hurt you. But the world is a different place. Please be careful about what you speak, whom you speak against, and what you wish for through your words. Just as you can insert a knife into someone and remove it, the injury remains despite countless apologies. People might say outwardly that they will forgive you, but in reality, they may not. I am not saying don't lay down your weapon completely, but act smartly!"

Understanding the gravity of his words, the young boy cast his gaze upon his father and hugged him!

Wrote with the help of

1. https://chat.openai.com/
2. https://ripplekindness.org/nails-in-the-fence/

CHAPTER XXIII

Purchasing need not always equal utilitarianism

A person from one country travels to another. He had consumed fruits and vegetables before, but this time, he decided to try out something new in the country. A vegetable vendor was selling colourful fruits and vegetables in a trolley shop. He decided to buy an item that was sold at the lowest price. After purchasing, he went happily to his room and consumed. Unfortunately, his eyes became watery. It turned out to be a variety of green chili. However, he continued to eat one or two even after knowing, in the thought process of inflicting a punishment for his mistake and not wasting the purchase or what might happen if he continued to eat. This could even be said of people who order food in hotels without knowing the spiciness for the first time but consume it because they have ordered it. Later, with maturity, they tell the spiciness level that has to be present in food or order proper food according to their desires.

The lesson learnt is that first-time mistakes happen in life, but if mistakes are not rectified and ego doesn't pave the way for humbleness and lessons learnt, life-long chili flakes have to be consumed without proper words of expression, whether by habit or by design. Also, one need not buy anything for the sake of trying something new or in the name of helping the economy or people through purchases or daring to explore the unknown because of advertisements. This has not only happened at the individual level but also even on large scales, where a complete expedition has gone wrong, and people have lost lives because they were unable to give up on the expedition at a certain stage due to the ego of their leader/captain of conquering the unknown. It has been told with the anecdotes of a team going to explore the Arctic Ocean and the Himalayas in *Paths of Glory'* by Jeffery Archer. Similarly, thoughts could go completely hayward when the idea that I have helped and am helping people gets to the head, and wrong notions about the self, a sense of superiority, a wrong ego or a wrong impression of the world and people around get imprinted in mind on a greater scale without humbleness. There are various economic models that argue about how consumerism improves the economy of the country, like Keynesian economics, which a student of economics might be able to discern, but an individual may not and need not necessarily think on a macro level and act on a micro level in the name of intelligence and large scale transformation is the ambition that could in spite of the sincerity, as argued may not be necessary as it could lead to personal glorification.

CHAPTER XXIV

Everything is not monism, dualism

Monism is a concept that attributes everything to a single entity, and dualism is a concept that attributes everything to two categories of things or principles. Being a layman and saying I am monistic or dualistic might make things look simple, but everything that does not need to be necessary is argued here from a mathematical perspective.

In mathematics, there are concepts called rings, fields and groups, which are part of abstract algebra, also known as modern algebra. There are some beautiful video demonstrations of how what looks like totally dissimilar figures are, in a way, geometrically the same via some transformations. So, the question is, in organic chemistry, there are many carbon compounds. Are all the chemical compounds the same because they are composed of carbon atoms? Can one structure be said to be similar to another? Everything can be converted to gold in the view of alchemy. Each geometrical figure or a chemical compound may look rigid but, via some transformations, may be made to look like another structure or another compound, but it will reach its ground state at one point or another; if it has a mind is unique, they have minds and have certain degrees of freedom in space, i.e. radical transformation to say a linear, homogenous, linked many chain structure or exhibiting polymorphism(many shapes) like and also not required but may sometimes happen through incremental steps over a long time period if patience and effort are shown aided by fewer distractions, in philosophical terms a kind of German idealism. For this geometrical shape to exhibit its mettle (strength), it is essential that it is aided by other geometrical shapes that are similar in existence in that space under natural circumstances.

Here comes the story of imitation: At one point in time, a simple geometrical figure that was happy with its existence thought of why not try to transform into some superior geometrical figure by aspiration. In layman's terms, it could be said as excelling in a field and achieving name and fame. It doesn't realise that the geometrical figure with which it is trying to compare and imitate has a different complexity and shape and exists in a different space. So, it tries to copy the transformations(actions) of that figure and expects the result of that geometrical transformational stability, acknowledgement, and happiness. The figure, which had undergone so many transformations from its beginning, slowly reaching its stability, even though it looks stable on the outside with the right credentials, seems to have lost its confidence on the inside. "Many strokes fell mighty oaks" happened. So, is it the fault of the system for showing the existence of various shapes and figures, or is it the fault of the geometrical shape to assume that it has its unique flexibility and perhaps may be possible for it to perform, transform such similar stunts and thereby achieve its stability, name, fame etc. or the fault of other shapes to have flexed their muscles to extraordinary lengths by desire, motivation, belief or perhaps other extraneous factors?

CHAPTER XXV

King Parikshit Maharaja – Some logic and Fatalism

Mahabharata is based on real events, which is one of the arguments I came across on social media. I believe what is telecasted on television is true. A psychological study tells us that we tend to organise events as if the memories are vivid. It's the same case. There have been many episodes, and I might not have watched everything in detail or would have ignored the details and craved for the heroism of the Pandavas and me being right, that is, having shown correct judgement in the end by placing faith in the right side and so on. But still, for the argument's sake, why did I believe the whole story to be true? I might have wanted to synthesise the data I gathered (through school education, television programmes, testimony(sabda) of others, including parents' epistemic belief, a way of leading life), and overall, I decided to be positive and happy about life, belief, there is a purpose in life and whatever been telecasted sounded reasonable to me, there is a divine being unknown to me and that the life has a force. This can be considered as a thesis. Now, say I have new data, what is quite the opposite, anti-thesis, getting the knowledge through the same means but of opposite in nature, the way I react will be different and will simply state that things are beyond my comprehension or might try to synthesise or both. In its extremity(overzealous, excess passion), everything becomes questionable, thereby spoiling the tranquillity within. I didn't believe in the stories I heard in childhood, as recent historical events and revolutions found an inkling and contemplation.

I bought Devdutt Patnaik's book, *Jaya, An Illustrated Retelling of the Mahabharata*, during the anti-thesis period, rejecting the stories as such, serving no real purpose and full of myth. I found it difficult to contain my thoughts and was carrying on the duties like a machine (Deus ex machina), as I had no idea what exactly I liked. Whatever is presented as an argument, I accepted, most likely except for myths and tradition, which I considered as outdated and have no relevance for no good reason or fault. (After a few tough years) Now, I am re-reading the book, and I suddenly delight in finding some data and sharing the details (blogging! I was at a loss for words then). The book is an anthology of events (small stories), and it begins with Parikshit Maharaja of Srimad Bhagavatam (which I started to read recently), who is cursed to be bitten by a snake within a week by a sage's disciple who saw the king make a mockery of his guru, by placing a dead snake over while he was on meditation. The king had requested the sage for water after having been on a hunting spree for a week and been thirsty, but the sage was not all ears then, as he had some deep mystic thoughts. If the incident is real, belief vs disbelief is the reason why the incident would have taken place. The king believed there was no such thing as deep meditation. And he is an Epicurean (happy) and pragmatic person. How could a rishi(sage) attain such perfection in his meditation? I, too, had the same doubt, while I was young, after having watched the idealism projected. I tried out meditation by standing on one leg, trying to live without food and water for a day or two, and trying to contain breathing activity. If the sage can, so can I, was my belief. There were also TV programmes like Junoon and Raja aur Rancho, where people doubted others. So, I tried to doubt real-life events, too, the credibility of people, and other possibilities. My mind is a tabla rasa (a blank slate), where I tried writing out everything. Calming my mind looks like an enormous challenge, as I don't want to lose time that I think might be wasted on others. I think I am the smartest person in the world, and I know every know-how. The king should have had the same belief; if the senses are real, then everyone should have the same senses;

he might or might not have tried out the other possibilities of how sages do meditation or worship. I worked with a logic which might be flawed due to the change in time periods, but still, it's a valid method of reasoning.

So, who is King Parikshit? He comes from the ancestry of Pandavas; he is the grandson of Arjuna and the son of Abhimanyu. It is mentioned in the book that he had put in plenty of safety around the kingdom and asked for every person or thing that came through the gate to be checked, but in spite of that, while he was about to eat some fruit, a serpent which had hidden in it, bit him from the inside. But Srimad Bhagavatam tells the story of the acceptance of fatalism and determinism, which King Parikshit had come to terms with having made a blunder and listened to the various stories from Mahabharata, from the sage's son, and thereby he attained a peaceful death on the seventh day. Which one could be the actual one?

CHAPTER XXVI

A logico-mathematical analysis cum ten different perspectives(10) of Tamil movie Kalki(1996)

This essay is an analysis of a movie and various perspectives of it. Any truth or an object for this matter can be presented to the senses in various perspectives and henceforth simply based on some subjective reality, which is a perspective, something real need not be forsaken.

To recall the movie synopsis from Wikipedia:

Chellammaa, a singer, is wedded to a chauvinistic, sadistic industrialist Prakash. She is unable to beget a child and hence is the target of hurting words from Prakash and his mother. When he prohibits her from singing, it is the last straw for her, and they divorce. Prakash marries Karpagam, a doormat wife, while Chellammaa stays single, with a cook named Kokila around to help her. Kalki works in an ad agency and is relentlessly pursued by coworker and model Paranjothi. She not only rejects him but also debunks love and sentiments. Chellammaa becomes friends with Kalki after a few encounters, and Kalki moves in as a paying guest. However, she strikes up a friendship with Prakash, and as a result of an affair with him, she ends up bearing his child. Kalki makes him understand what he is doing to his wife by treating him the way he treats his wife. During the time of delivery, Karpagam, with her lawyer, threatens Prakash that she is going to divorce him. However, upon realising the mistakes that he made, he says sorry to Karpagam and asks for a chance to change himself. She agrees with a condition not to hurt Kalki's child and also to live with Kalki. Prakash agrees to both the conditions. When they meet

Kalki and inform her of this, Kalki says that she does not want to live with them and that she is not ready to give the child to them. Before delivery, she meets Chellamma and informs him that she did live with Prakash to teach him a lesson. She had a child just for Chellamma and left the child with Chellamma after delivery. After that, society is not ready to accept her, so she goes to Paranjothi, who is waiting for her and confesses her love for him.

Story Plot as Propositions (Philosophical logic) and Set theory notations:

There is a difference between language and mathematics; where language succeeds in bringing in the emotion, mathematics might not be able to, but where mathematics succeeds in bringing in the truth, words may not succeed due to the interference of emotion. As drama is about catharsis(expression of emotion), words are required in addition, but in order to avoid being judgemental, the names are avoided, and A, B, C, and D are used for characters.

Propositional Statements:

P1: A, belonging to the M category (here gender), marries and verbally abuses B, belonging to the F category.

P2: B is dominant, and so argues back, but no luck, gets divorced.

P3: A, still belonging to M, marries C and then continues verbal abuses, and C is non-dominant. Therefore, it is a one-sided tirade.

P4: B accidentally passes this information to D (belonging to F), who is supposed to represent super-dominant, interfering in activities outside the knowledge scope

P5: B doesn't employ D for revenge against F, nor does D have any information on A, but D does those actions by marrying, having a child, and abusing A.

Story Conclusion: A gets a good lesson on how to run the family affairs and promises to treat equal the members of the other class well and an undesirable quality of A has got suppressed and also "Movies work on magic, not logic!"

M-Category, there happens to be Male gender, F - Another category and here happens to be Female gender

For *Kalki* Story Correlation and **Coherence**:

A - Prakash, played by Prakash Raj

B- Chellamāl, played by Geetha

C- Karpagam, played by Renuka

D- Kalki, played by Shruti

Director: K. Balachander (KB)

In P1 to P5, when certain sequences are changed, a different story is formed. For example, what happens if A and B approach D for help and D takes revenge (Ladies vs Rickie Bahl, Johny Tucker Must Die)? In P1 to P5, what happens when A cheats B, C and D for money (Naan Avan Illai, Ladies vs Rickie Bahl)? What happens when A cheats B, C and D for fun is that A happens to be a playboy (Bachna Ae Haseeno, Theeradha Vilayaatu Pillai). So, having A, B, C, and D helps in understanding how some part of the world works!

In mathematical set notations (as per Set theory), the class and items in it could be represented as $A \in M$, B & $C \in F$.

Brief Abstract:

As per Hindu Puranas, Kalki stands for the 10th god who will destroy the world that is in existence, as the whole world is supposed to be full of injustice, based on popular opinion or prevailing events which God sees. As luck or God, whichever way to put it, would have it, the Qualitative Analytical (QA) perspective has ten different perspectives. I searched for the gender of Kalki's avatar but couldn't find any convincing answers. In the movie, the character is a female, and it could be inferred as one who brought an end to a male-dominated life, which could be extended to society as well based on generosity. If someone asks why generosity is required for the extension to society, they have to read the QA part completely. It could be argued the noble intentions of the director and his crew, but I beg to differ based on various viewpoints, as the majority doesn't support the extension to society at large. It need not apply to the readers however.

Some Qualitative Analytical (QA) perspectives:

Fact: A (Prakash) and B (Chellamāl) before the divorce, were married for four years.

QA 1: An instinctive cum confusion perspective:

When A starts dominating B, B should have counterattacked and fought immediately. By 2023 standards, B should have left A immediately in the first year of marriage. But, some confusion or some impression or some thought process in B, or some faith/ fear or some attraction made B stick to the marriage with A. Like said, it could be faith/fear, which could be rewritten as things will get better in the future or said as faith in the marriage system/ insecurity in the outside world. But like Pavlov's conditioning, some years of humiliation and some trite/innovative responses possibly didn't help B resolve the matter. What if A had stopped dominating

B after two years of marriage? Would B have forgiven A for having done such actions? Or did the movie create scenes extravagantly, portraying certain aspects of a man that created problems for him and others?

QA 2: An audience perspective:

A particular movie scene might be attractive, and a sweet spot may be found in memory due to the good enactment of the character. But when a person representing one gender or class abuses a member of another gender, simply on the basis that the gender or class has less prerogatives in the society, possibly at some point of time in history. An individual who might call himself liberal, free-spirited, an audience, an artist, a sadist or any other might view with pleasure such scenes without knowing or analysing the scene in much detail. The scene from a constricted or broader viewpoint, whichever way to put it forward, might stand as a reminder that such mistakes should be avoided in the future. But how often will a person get that reminder- a random combination of free will and some other extraneous factors?

QA 3: A bold but peaceful feminist perspective:

B finally found some courage to leave A, following all the legal protocols. Why was B tied to A in such a relationship? Why will a person leave without any compensation after having been humiliated? Even when A is rich, why would B react in such a way? Money is not everything, and it is not a knee-jerk reaction after years of patience towards humiliation. B, too, is rich and feels the need for protection through laws. Also, it is a possibility that the prevailing laws at that time favoured men possibly, so she didn't want to risk much and wanted a peaceful resolution. As her husband is not shown as a goon, a rowdy, or a powerful man, she wants a peaceful resolution to be left out.

QA 4: A gaming perspective:

Here, there are 2 opposing forces: male chauvinism(excessive support for one group) and feminism(the advocacy of equal rights for women). It is not the question of how or why these 2 forces are necessary. They somehow have sprouted out. An intelligent, clever answer, like altogether averting mistakes by leading a serene, wise life, will not be accepted by a gamer. There are 2 powerful forces: A takes for male chauvinism, and B, C, and D for feminism. A plays Mortal Kombat/WWE kind with B and wins a tough fight; A then plays the same game with C, who happens to be a weak opponent and manages to play with that opponent continuously for a long time. D, having seen all the nuisances done by A, challenges B and then crushes/wins over B. For better understanding, A has some powers $\{P4, Q4, R4, S4\}$, B $\{P3, Q3, R3, S3\}$, C = $\{P2, Q2, R2, S2\}$, D= $\{P5, Q5, R5, S5\}$ and $P5>P4>P3>P2>P1$ and similarly for others, P, Q, R, S are some powers and D is able to overthrow A and A is able to overthrow B and C. B, C and D didn't fight with each other.

QA5: A soul perspective:

A, B, C, D are all parts of a single person's soul. A(a bright person) is an unhappy individual for some reason and, because of that, shows dislike for his dear quality(B), which he was married to/born with. So B left him, citing the unhappy and abusive relationship. So, At that time of crisis, A needs calmness and should have thought of what is needed. But A couldn't do that due to some obsession or some clinging. So A, without full commitment or happiness, marries what his mother thought would be apt for him: good character. A gets good character(C) and gets going for a while, but it couldn't fit his profile/suit. He can't fit in with that perfection, dedication, and subordination after some time, and so he grows unhappy. He then tries to find a character of his liking, a nomad, a playboy with a vigilante lifestyle and tries to find prey in the outside world but somehow gets into a self-referential paradox, where the enemy is himself on the other side, thereby wanting to get out sooner by tying up with good character and conduct.

QA6: A secret agency perspective:

Entering into an emotional relationship and breaking from a relationship is difficult unless the person is well-trained in the affairs. Since the movie revolves around the title character(D), who appears to be a normal person who is not trained to handle such affairs, the assumption is going to be the same. So when the character marries a person who was twice married before, with the big revelation in the end that it was for revenge for the atrocities committed by that person against the feminine gender in the first two marriages, with all the gripping music, editing and enactment, it looks convincing argument for a naïve person. But honestly, a person cannot justify prolonged emotional actions/drama under the cloud of rationality unless trained well in the art of deception.

QA7: From Martin Scorsese's *Shutter Island* (2010) perspective:

Martin Scorsese's *Shutter Island* (2010) movie works on the premise that it is the detective who is actually the patient. Similarly, here, D could actually be a patient who has some wrong or narrow perspectives about the world. Here, D is shown as a feminist, a libertarian and an iconoclast(one who attacks cherished opinions or beliefs). Can an iconoclast stay as an iconoclast for a long time without any external support, proper guidance, or groups/ communities? Can a person who has tested the lines of poverty and has no means of survival stay calm and maintain composure at all times? Does the decisions taken by that person be said to have been made by a sane person? There must be a hidden psyche built within that person, with all the issues, even though the person sports a happy look. Somehow, the person was identified was given testing times, but the person failed to get the notion that utilitarianism (benefitting maximum people altruism(disinterested and selfless concern for the well-being of others), feminism, and libertarianism can go hand in hand with personal liberty and a better understanding of people, society than a narrow constrained viewpoint. So, there is an iconoclast hidden within that person to find out the flaws within the system. What provoked the person to be living under such strenuous circumstances? Could the person have lived better? Were there any external factors or intrinsic factors such as family circumstances, some failures, or some quests that have not been achieved? There is a thirst, a longing for happiness, there is a display of bold effrontery, and it is possible that the latter could have caused the former.

QA 8: A quantum psychological/dream perspective:

A, B, C, D are atoms in a quantum world. Quantum entanglement is a bizarre, counterintuitive phenomenon that explains how 2 subatomic particles can be intimately linked to each other even if separated by billions of light-years of space. (Wikipedia) Here, entanglement will be used for interaction. A got entangled with B, then A with C, and then D got entangled with B and then got entangled with A. D tried to play super-atom, determine A's interaction with C, transferred certain energy in the process, spiralled out of its trajectory and therefore tried to reach one of its previous stable states by going back to its previous job and evergreen lover, who has not changed a bit in spite of having acted in movies and had a prolonged gap, which is a good psychological dream to have.

QA 9: A theological perspective:

Shaktism is the worship of the Hindu goddess Shakti (Power or Energy). Adi Shankara and others worshipped and preached the worship of Goddess. In various religions, it is called by various names. So when such a feminine energy was not only not worshipped, but treated with disparity, the divine intervened in worldly affairs and resolved a problem. So, here, D is a goddess.

QA 10: A lesson for the future perspective:

D thinks of the self as superior, and so the self as superior by associating the mind with higher ideals and values, when in fact, the self is not confident and weak because of having ignored the responsibilities or by some actions such as resigning from a job or some uncertainty such as economic, when paying for room service was difficult or uncertain views about the world/life/God or some particular matter/issues that clouded the mind. Resigning the job and getting an affair with a person who is made to spend lavishly by writing an enormous amount of cheques, only to later reveal/justify that it is for some revenge course of action for his past deed and then go onto the previous state of living may happen for anyone, who tries to balance out rationality with intuitionism/belief. It is a common trap, and a person who is not philosophically trained or has discipline may try to poke his nose into other affairs outside the scope.

Conclusion:

People might have suffered and blues (sorrow) bequeathed due to ignorance/mistakes, but add a few strokes of smiles, songs, and boosting words; it is a caravan entertainment package with hidden meanings. It is an abstract art, a representation of platonic(non-physical, intellectual) work, one of the philosopher's stones carved for the 21st century. It is to be noted that, though B and C reprove the method of D, they finally give assent and praise D, which could be a director's touch, a brushstroke of ending things well in movies, mostly impractical in real life, as a person's sanity is tested in those aspects.

Some Memorable Quotes

"Man acts as though he were the shaper and master of language, while in fact language remains the master of man."

• Martin Heidegger

"You believe in a book that has talking animals, wizards, witches, demons, sticks turning into snakes, burning bushes, food falling from the sky, people walking on water, and all sorts of magical, absurd and primitive stories, and you say that we are the ones that need help?"

• Mark Twain

"Some cause happiness wherever they go; others whenever they go."
"The only difference between the saint and the sinner is that every saint has a past, and every sinner has a future."

• Oscar Wilde

"An expert is a person who has made all the mistakes that can be made in a very narrow field."

• Niels Bohr, Nobel Prize laureate in Physics

"Mathematics is the bold luxury of pure reason, one of the few that remain today."

• Robert Musil, Austrian Philosopher

"There is nothing more deceptive than an obvious fact. Life is infinitely stranger than anything which the mind of man could invent. We would not dare to conceive the things which are really mere commonplaces of existence."

• Sherlock Holmes

"If one advances confidently in the direction of his dreams, and endeavors to live the life which he has imagined, he will meet with a success unexpected in common hours."

• Henry David Thoreau

Thanks for reading!

www.ingramcontent.com/pod-product-compliance
Lightning Source LLC
Chambersburg PA
CBHW032000140726
47988CB00019B/2922